OUT TO LUNCH!

Make Me Laugh!

OUT TO LUNCH!

jokes about food

by Peter & Connie Roop / pictures by Joan Hanson

Lerner Publications Company · Minneapolis

*To our families, who find their trips to the trough
full-filling*

This book is available in two editions:
Library binding by Lerner Publications Company
Soft cover by First Avenue Editions
241 First Avenue North
Minneapolis, Minnesota 55401

Library of Congress Cataloging-in-Publication Data

Roop, Peter.
  Out to lunch!

  (Make me laugh!)
  Summary: A selection of jokes about food, cooking, baking, and eating.
  1. Gastronomy—Anecdotes, facetiae, satire, etc.
2. Wit and humor, Juvenile. [1. Food—Wit and humor. 2. Jokes] I. Roop,
Connie. II. Hanson, Joan, ill.
III. Title. IV. Series.
PN6231.G35R6   1984   818'.5402   84-4416
ISBN 0-8225-0983-0 (lib. bdg.)
ISBN 0-8225-9552-4 (pbk.)

Manufactured in the United States of America

          4   5   6   7   8   9   10   94   93   92   91   90   89

Q: Why are bananas so attractive?

A: They have plenty of a-peel.

Q: What food is never hot?
A: Chili.

Q: When is a potato like a bad idea?
A: When it's half-baked.

Q: What kind of flour is used to make dog biscuits?
A: Collie-flour!

Q: What kind of fruit do fish like?
A: Water-melon.

Q: What did the caveman have for lunch?
A: A club sandwich!

Q: What did the potato say to the potato chip?
A: "You're a chip off the old block."

Pat: Joe the butcher tells such funny jokes!
Nat: Yeah, he's a real cut-up!

Fred: Did you hear about the boy who died
from eating 50 pancakes?
Ted: How waffle!

Q: What food stays hot no matter how cold it is?
A: A pepper.

Sally: More alphabet soup, please.

Mom: But you've already had five bowls!

Sally: I know, but I want to pass my spelling test!

Q: Why do cows dance?

A: To make their milkshakes.

Q: What is an elephant's favorite food?

A: Squash.

Q: What letter do cooks like to bake?
A: They like to cook-"E's."

Q: What did the mayonnaise say to the refrigerator?

A: "Close the door, I'm dressing!"

Q: What day is the best day to drink milk?

A: Thirst-day.

Q: If bread had feet, what kind of shoes would it wear?

A: Loafers.

Q: What fruit did Noah eat on the Ark?
A: Pairs (pears).

Q: What is a sailor's favorite food?
A: Navy beans.

Q: What's the best day to eat ice cream?
A: Sundae.

Q: What is a mango's favorite dance?
A: The mango tango!

Q: How does a turkey eat his food?
A: He gobbles it.

Q: What is a monster's favorite dessert?
A: Ice scream.

Q: Where is the best place to eat
along the highway?
A: Wherever there's a fork in the road.

Q: What side of an apple is the reddest?
A: The outside.

Q: What's the best place to keep a square meal?
A: In a lunch box.

Q: What seven letters did the girl say when she opened the refrigerator?

A: "O-I-C-U-R-M-T."

Bill: Can you cook an egg in your pajamas?
Will: Yes, but it's easier to use a pan!

Q: What's a lazy person's favorite food?
A: Meat loaf.

Mother: Jason, why are you eating hay?
Jason: You always say I eat like a horse!

Q: What fruit do sheep like to eat?
A: Baa-nanas.

Q: What did the watermelon say after the honeydew proposed marriage?
A: "Yes, but I cantaloupe!" (Can't elope.)

Q: What does a cannibal call his guests?
A: Dinner!

Q: What's a bully's favorite drink?
A: Punch.

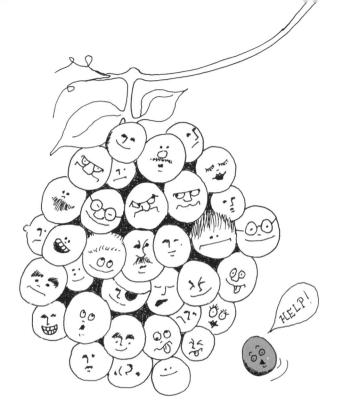

Q: Why are grapes never lonely?

A: Because they always hang around
in bunches.

Q: What did one potato chip say to the other?
A: "Want to go for a dip?"

Q: Why is a baker never rich?
A: Because he always kneads dough!

Knock, knock. Who's there?
Lettuce. Lettuce who?
Lettuce in!

Q: What do you call a funny pickle?
A: A silly dilly.

Q: When does a pig taste the best?
A: When it's bakin' (bacon).

Q: What's a coward's favorite food?
A: Chicken!

Q: What did one strawberry say to the other?
A: "You've got to help me, I'm in a jam."

Q: What kind of fruit do you find on ships?
A: "Naval" oranges.

Q: What's a cook's favorite magazine?
A: *Eater's Digest.*

Q: Why did the ice cream dive into the pool?
A: It wanted to take a dip.

Q: How do you know when a turkey is full?
A: When it's stuffed!

Q: What do you get when you cross a chicken
with a puppy?

A: Pooched eggs!

Q: Why did the explorer try to stay calm when he met the cannibal?

A: He didn't want to get into a stew!

Q: Why did the baker stop making doughnuts?

A: He got tired of the hole business.

Q: What do you get when you mix chocolate with potatoes?

A: Chocolate chips!

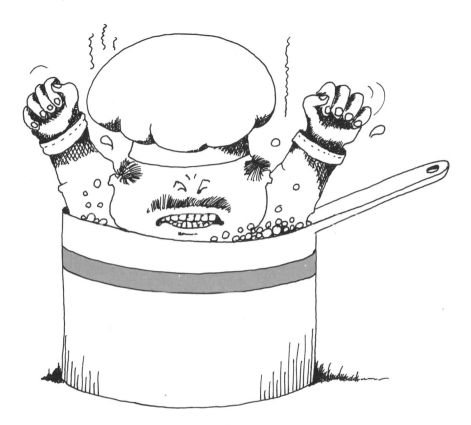

Q: What happens to a cook when he's angry?
A: He gets boiling mad.

ABOUT THE AUTHORS

PETER AND CONNIE ROOP have enjoyed sharing jokes with students in the United States and Great Britain. When not joking around, Peter and Connie write books and articles. Traveling, camping, and reading with their children, Sterling and Heidi, are their favorite pastimes. Both graduates of Lawrence University, the Roops now live in Appleton, Wisconsin.

ABOUT THE ARTIST

JOAN HANSON lives with her husband and two sons in Afton, Minnesota. Her distinctive, deliberately whimsical pen-and-ink drawings have illustrated more than 30 children's books. Ms. Hanson is also an accomplished weaver. A graduate of Carleton College, Hanson enjoys tennis, skiing, sailing, reading, traveling, and walking in the woods surrounding her home.

Make Me Laugh!

101 ANIMAL JOKES
101 FAMILY JOKES
101 KNOCK-KNOCK JOKES
101 MONSTER JOKES
101 SCHOOL JOKES
101 SPORTS JOKES
CAT'S OUT OF THE BAG!
GO HOG WILD!
GOING BUGGY!
GRIN AND BEAR IT!
IN THE DOGHOUSE!

LET'S CELEBRATE!
OUT TO LUNCH!
SPACE OUT!
STICK OUT YOUR TONGUE!